The Army of Truth

The Army of Truth

~

SELECTED POEMS BY
HENRIK WERGELAND

*In the historic fight to obtain equal rights for
Jews in nineteenth-century Norway*

Edited by Ragnhild Galtung

Translated by Anne Born, G. M. Gathorne-Hardy, and I. Grøndahl

Introduction by Dagne Groven Myhren

THE UNIVERSITY OF WISCONSIN PRESS

The University of Wisconsin Press
1930 Monroe Street, 3rd Floor
Madison, Wisconsin 53711-2059
uwpress.wisc.edu

3 Henrietta Street
London WC2E 8LU, England
eurospanbookstore.com

Printed in the United States of America

Library of Congress Cataloging-in-Publication Data
Wergeland, Henrik Arnold, 1808–1845.
[Engelskc lods. English]
The Army of Truth : selected poems : in the historic fight to obtain
equal rights for Jews in nineteenth-century Norway / by Henrik Wergeland;
edited by Ragnhild Galtung ; translated by Anne Born,
G. M. Gathorne-Hardy, and I. Grøndahl ;
introduction by Dagne Groven Myhren.
p. cm.
ISBN 0-299-18530-3 (cloth : alk. paper)
I. Galtung, Ragnhild. II. Title.
PT8939.E37 E5413   2003
839.8'216—dc21   2003002165

ISBN 978-0-299-18534-3 (pbk. : alk. paper)
ISBN 978-0-299-18533-6 (e-book)

Frontispiece: I. W. Tegner & Kattendorff, *Henrik Wergeland,* lithograph after
daguerreotype, National Library of Norway, Oslo Division,
Picture Collection

The Army of Truth is a publication of Thanks To Scandinavia, an educational fund and an institute of the American Jewish Committee. For more information about the work of Thanks To Scandinavia, contact

Thanks To Scandinavia
165 East 56th Street
New York, New York 10022

Phone (212) 891-1403
Fax (212) 838-2120
Tts@ajc.org
www.ThanksToScandinavia.org

Thanks To Scandinavia is a nonprofit organization

Table of Contents

Foreword

Henrik Wergeland, Norway's beloved poet, is also remembered for his ardent work in support of Jews. I am pleased to present this volume of his groundbreaking poems translated, some for the first time, into English, in order to make his historic contribution to humanistic ethics accessible to a wider audience.

Henrik Wergeland found it a disgrace that the Norwegian constitution of 1814 did not allow Jews to enter the country. His efforts to change Norwegian law accordingly were finally vindicated in 1851, six years after his death, when Jewish and Jesuit immigration was legalized.

The twelve poems in this publication are part of Wergeland's campaign for Jewish rights. Some of the poems have been selected from *Poems*, published by Gyldendal Norsk Forlag, Oslo, and Hodder & Stoughton, Ltd., London, in 1929, and translated by G. M. Gathorne-Hardy ("Follow the Call," "The Maple and the Pine," "A Voice in the Wilderness," "On the Sick Bed," "The Army of Truth") and I. Grøndahl ("The Thistledown Gatherer," "Christmas Eve," "The Three"), both of Great Britain. Three poems have been newly translated for this collection: "Briar Shoots," "The Jewess," and "The Women at the Graveyard," as well as the prose portion of the poem "Wanton Weeds."

Dr. Dagne Groven Myhren, assistant professor of Nordic literature at the University of Oslo and one of Norway's foremost specialists on Wergeland and his works, selected the poems to be included in this collection. Dr. Groven Myhren also wrote the introduction and chronology for this publication.

Anne Born, a well-known translator who resides in England, has re-translated the poems from the 1929 collection into more modern language and done original translations of the pieces added to this compilation. In addition to being a translator, Ms. Born is also a poet in her own right and has won numerous awards and received recognition in both fields. She has done exemplary work in translating these beautiful verses.

This publication has been supported by Thanks To Scandinavia, a scholarship fund founded in 1963 by Danish entertainer Victor Borge and New York attorney Richard Netter, who has served as its president of the organization since its founding. As director of The Norway-America Association, one of my greatest inspirations and pleasures for more than thirty-six years has been the cooperation with Thanks To Scandinavia and Richard Netter. It is remarkable that since its founding, the organization has raised an endowment of $6 million to provide scholarships for young Scandinavians for studies and research in the United States as a token of gratitude for assistance given Jews during World War II. Thanks To Scandinavia also sponsors diverse educational programs in the United States, Scandinavia, and Israel.

In February 1998, the Polish-born Israeli Pessah Ostashinsky received a copy of a Thanks To Scandinavia book entitled *Norway's Response to the Holocaust* by the late New York City College professor Samuel Abrahamson. Inspired by the book, he broached the idea of a publication of Wergeland's translated poems with Thanks To Scandinavia. Unfortunately, Mr. Ostashinky died in November 1998, too soon to see the fruits of his recommendation realized.

Thanks To Scandinavia president Richard Netter is known in Norway for his tremendous success in building Thanks To Scandinavia into a significant and perpetual fund. In addition, he richly deserves recognition for his understanding of the value of Henrik Wergeland's poems in their vital historical context as well as today, and for his unfailing encouragement during the making of this publication, which has finally turned the idea into a reality.

His Majesty King Olav V, at an audience at the Royal Palace in Oslo in April 1982, bestowed Mr. Netter with Knight First Class of the Order of St. Olav, which was awarded him for his humanitarian services and the promotion of Norwegian-American relations. Similar awards have been presented to him and Mr. Borge, whose recent passing we mourn, from the other Scandinavian countries.

The year 2001 was proclaimed by Secretary-General Kofi Annan as "United Nations Year of Dialogue among Nations," based on equality among all nations and peoples regardless of their race, color, creed, and national origin. This vision was one strongly held by Henrik Wergeland 150 years ago. His hope for a better tomorrow for future generations was based on the need for tolerance, understanding, and mutual respect. His generosity and liberality for his fellow men is abundantly evident in his poems.

We in Norway are also grateful that some of Henrik Wergeland's poems in this way may gain a greater readership. His ideas were universal, but he lacked a language that could introduce the poems to the larger world. This is an attempt to remedy that.

Ragnhild Galtung
Director 1958–96
The Norway-America Association

Introduction

Henrik Arnold Wergeland lived and wrote in the stirring period after the Napoleonic wars when Norway was laying its foundations as an independent nation. His brilliant talent left a lasting impression on Norway's cultural and social life. In the powerful cosmological poem *Creation, Man and Messiah* (1830), in which he describes his philosophy of life and the world, he stakes out his course. The work has its roots in antiquity, the recent past, and the present—i.e., in the eighteenth and early nineteenth centuries. When he was revising the work on his deathbed, he composed much of his political testament in a newly written utopian epilogue, "The Spiritual Resurrection of Jesus."

During his short life Wergeland devoted much of his energy to converting his poetic and political ideas into practical action. He threw himself into the work of educating the people and establishing social services. He showed concern for the poor and oppressed in other lands as well. He supported the celebration of Norwegian Constitution Day on May 17, worked to establish independent Norwegian art and culture, and encouraged writers to create "jewels" (i.e., literature) out of the living Norwegian language. It pleased him that his friend, the internationally renowned violin virtuoso, Ole Bull, found inspiration in Norwegian folk music.

It is hardly an exaggeration to say that Wergeland himself created a complete literature on his own. He holds a place among the most distinguished poets of Scandinavia. He had considerable talent both for drama and the epic, but at heart he was a lyric poet with an unusual gift for imagery. He had the ability to assemble and retain several perspectives in one grasp. This makes him difficult to translate. Had he written in a major world language he would undoubtedly have had a place among the great romantic poets of liberty. A present-day Norwegian lyric poet, Arnold Eidslott, calls him "Pushkin's brother," and his father,

Nicolai Wergeland, characterized him as "the Norwegian Byron or the Norwegian Pushkin, or the Norwegian Victor Hugo." At difficult moments he could well have wished for a more generous milieu and a more universal language to write in. This is apparent from "Follow the Call!" But this poem also shows how, in spite of everything, he came to terms with working inside the narrow confines available to him.

His tireless commitment to the Jewish cause led to two of his poetry collections, *The Jew* (1842) and *The Jewess* (1844), being distributed among Jewish communities beyond the borders of Norway. Some of these poems are among the best known in Norwegian literature, such as "The Army of Truth," "On the Sick Bed," "Follow the Call," and the epic poem "Christmas Eve." In recent years the latter has been broadcast by Norwegian radio every Christmas Eve, read by the distinguished actor, poet, and Wergeland admirer Claes Gill. Even today it makes a compelling impression.

Henrik Wergeland was born on June 17, 1808, in the southernmost town of Norway, Kristiansand, where at that time his father was a teacher. Later, Wergeland senior became a priest and dean. Henrik's mother, Alette Thaulow from Kristiansand, came from a family of civil servants with a great fondness for the arts. As a young woman she acted for the local dramatic society to general acclaim. Her father came from a farming family in western Norway. He had worked his way up from humble beginnings and taken an excellent theological degree. He was an industrious writer, and in 1810 was accorded high praise for a work arguing for the establishment of a Norwegian university. His proposal was adopted in 1811 and the university came into being in 1813. By 1814 he was a leading member of the national assembly at Eidsvoll that gave Norway its own constitution.

In 1817, when Henrik was nine years old, the family left Kristiansand and moved to Eidsvoll, where the father had been given a position. The historic country town in the heart of southeast Norway, about sixty kilometers from Kristiania (present-day Oslo), thus became Henrik Wergeland's native district, and a place to which he liked to return, in his writing as well. During his student years and afterward he spent periods living at home at the vicarage. Henrik Wergeland took his degree in theology in 1829. He was a controversial figure in Norwegian society due both to his personality and his ideas—and was never appointed to an ecclesiastical post. He studied medicine for a year or two, but took no examination. For a time he edited the journal of the opposition, *Statsborgeren* (The Citizen). He also filled a deputy post as an amanuensis at the university library in the capital. In 1839 the king, Carl Johan, offered him a grant from his personal funds, a kind of state stipend, almost as a plaster for the wound he had inflicted on Wergeland by never allowing him to hold even a very modest parish. Henrik Wergeland defined the grant as payment for his educational work. However, it enabled him to marry.

Henrik Wergeland did not obtain a permanent appointment until 1840, when he was appointed director of the National Archives, the first post of its kind in the young nation, an office he assiduously maintained. In May 1844 he fell ill. During the course of his fourteen months' confinement to bed he wrote some of his most beautiful poems. One of the last projects he completed was his memoir, *Hassel-nødder* (Hazelnuts), published a week after his death. In it he describes his travels in England and France in 1831. Under the heading "The Real Initiators of the Emancipation of the Jews" he recalls a memorable meeting with two Moroccan Jews in Paris: "I felt humbled before them as if I stood before two of the progenitors of humankind or before Abraham and Melchizedek, under whose tent only the one true God was worshiped."

During the declaration of peace in Kiel on January 14, 1814, it was decreed that Norway, which had been united with Denmark for more than 400 years, should be ceded to Sweden as a recompense for the latter's loss of Finland to Russia. In Norway people were shocked at this decree. But it turned out to provide new potential for the country. Action was taken quickly. Before the union with Sweden was established Norway had given herself a constitution. A national assembly was elected and met at Eidsvoll on April 10, 1814, and by May 17 the constitution of the Kingdom of Norway had come into existence. On the same day, the Danish prince Christian Frederik was proclaimed king. He reigned for only a few months. The union with Sweden was inevitable, but the Eidsvoll constitution was a substantial contribution toward the achievement for Norway of a substantial degree of independence. The Norwegian constitution was one of the most liberal in the world for its time, and built on eighteenth-century ideas of the distribution of power, the sovereignty of the people, and human rights.

The work of liberation carried out in 1814 was of decisive importance for Henrik Wergeland, who liked to describe himself as the "older brother of the constitution by six years." He had a high regard for the constitution, and wrote *Norges Konstitutions Historie* (History of the Constitution of Norway, 1842–43). But he wanted a revision on one point. In the name of freedom of religion and tolerance he demanded a change in clause 2, which refused Jews entrance to the country. In his opinion the clause was incompatible with the general spirit of the constitution. In 1839 he put forward a well-grounded proposal for the constitutional change. He closely pursued the case for a number of years, right up to his death, in fact. He acquired a wide-ranging knowledge of the position of the Jews, partly through corresponding with Jews in other countries, and contributed a great deal to the creation and maintaining of opinion with works such as "Indlæg i Jødesagen" (A Contribution to the Jewish Cause, 1841) and "Jødesagen i Det norske Storthing" (The Jewish Cause in the Norwegian Parliament, 1842), and not least through his poetry. Thanks to Wergeland's efforts the cause, in spite of one or two delays, made great progress in his lifetime. But not until 1851, six years after the death of Wergeland, was the Jewish clause rescinded.

With *The Jew* and *The Jewess*, Wergeland desired to work for tolerance and combat intolerance and prejudice, especially prejudice against the Jews. The Scandinavian term *fordom* derives from Latin *prejudicium*, a judgment that is pronounced hastily, without sufficient knowledge of a matter. The concept of "prejudice" occurs in the Norwegian original both in "Sandhedens Armee" (translated as "Error") and in "Kvinderne paa Kirkegaarden" (translated as "Prejudice"). Wergeland describes the poems with a Jewish theme as "blossoming bramble twigs," an expression holding associations with beauty, love, and suffering.

The Jew is dedicated to "The Parliament of Norway" and came out during the year when an amendment to the constitution was to be voted upon for the first time. *The Jewess* opens with the beautiful poem "On the Sick Bed," which shows the grievous physical and psychological sufferings under which these poems were brought into being. But in only one of the other poems can illness be glimpsed, in the depiction of the wounded golden eagle in "Follow the Call!"

The introductory poem in *The Jew*, "The Army of Truth," is concerned with words and the world, with the poet's battle for awareness, light, and truth against a dense spiritual darkness that expresses itself in ignorance, lies, and prejudice. The theme is central to all of Wergeland's writing, and readily apparent in other poems dedicated to the Jewish cause, as for instance "Follow the Call!"

In "The Army of Truth" the poet encourages his wretched but brave army of poetic words to strike down the army of black prejudices (translated as "the black-clad guards of error") who have entrenched themselves outside the temple and thus implicitly also in the hearts of men. The truth tempts the miserably poor, and there is a danger that the world, as so many times before, will reject it. The allusions in the prologue to the Gospel of St. John are plain, particularly if one bears in mind that light is a symbol of the Logos. (Cf. "And the light shineth in Darkness, and the Darkness comprehendeth it not," John, 1.5). The victory one can hope for is that of martyrdom. But truth, despite everything, is a child of the Lord. The words of poetry are its knights, and they are exhorted to fight with their visors open. (In the translation: "Forward though, you feeble lines / Words are armies!"). The aim is that truth shall liberate the hearts of men for love, so that they flourish and become generous. The light rays of understanding will literally disperse the darkness of lies and prejudices that make the heart narrow and niggardly, and build bright dwellings for the truth within: "In the end the hearts of men / will be your victorious home," the lines run hopefully.

"Follow the Call" points among other things to the depressing fact that Europe is divided into sects with a mutual hatred of each other. But it ends in a hard-earned faith that the words of poetry, which are in accord with "Our Lord's own voice" and the creative powers in the world, will slowly contribute to progress, to "the dawn of better days."

In the Norwegian original "Follow the Call" is provided with a prose epilogue, not included in this selection, that links the poem more directly to the Jewish question. The poet imagines that "love will spread like an invisible fire" from a single woman weeping over the evicted Jew, to other women, and so from them to their men. He exclaims: "O, there is no wailing as long as one heart is open." The epilogue alludes to the Bible story of John the Baptist and elucidates the other biblical allusions in the poem. And this epilogue points further to the utopia in the revised version of *Creation, Man and Messiah*, written only a couple of months later. The utopia makes it clear that development toward an earthly kingdom of peace is dependent on human beings' apprehending and practicing that which is found to bring conscious light in Wergeland's three key concepts of truth, freedom, and love. They also form, as should have appeared, a sounding board in "The Army of Truth."

Like "Follow the Call," "Røst I Ørkenen" (Voice in the Wilderness) alludes to John the Baptist. Here, moreover, Christians are taken to task in striking metaphors for their hardness of heart, indeed for ungodliness! This same thing occurs too in a different fashion in "Juleaftenen" (Christmas Eve), which echoes the Christmas story. The old Jewish tramp, Jacob, who travels around the border regions between Norway and Sweden, shows himself to be more "Christian" than the Christians who drive him and the child he is trying to rescue out into the cold on Christmas Eve itself.

The theme of eviction is also central to "Kaadt Ukrudt" (Wanton Weeds). The aim is to demonstrate how self-contradictory Norwegian law and the Lutheran Church (the sunflower) are when they permit even devil worshipers to enter the country but debar the Jew (the modest mignonette)!

The dialogue "Jeg Er Nu Saadan Jeg" (The Maple and the Pine) is another variation on the theme of ostracism. The tone is good-natured but the message cannot be ignored. A maple and a pine are made to represent two typical attitudes toward foreigners (the bees, a metaphor for the Jews) who wish to settle in the forest (the land of Norway). The strongest arguments are put forward by the hospitable maple, while the pine, which basically lacks argument, asserts its special nature and need for solitude. The maple considers that the industrious and friendly bees will make a positive contribution to the community (national economy), and is therefore happy to welcome them:

The dish love gives is free to all,
though with no pomp and pride
it pays again and yet again
with coin of gratitude.

In many of the poems Wergeland emphasizes the high moral standards, diligence, and tolerance of Jewish women. He probably thinks it is greatly to their credit that they managed to preserve their culture despite the fact that "all the roses are destroyed, / roots wide scattered." In Wergeland's opinion they have values to bring to Norwegian society, but here love must be in command, "not the roaring Lion of Law," as we read in "Briar Shoots," with a play on the image of a lion on the Norwegian national coat of arms.

In the poem "The Jewess" the brilliant Rachel is held up before "these Nordic men," those who are to pronounce judgment on the Jewish question. She is at one and the same time an Eve from before the Fall and a Mary figure, and represents Jewish femininity at its finest. When she uncovers her face she shines with a light of awareness that makes all arguments superfluous.

In the outstanding poem "The Women in the Churchyard" it is a Jewess who has the decisive word. Here, as in "The Three," the message is religious tolerance, akin to the ideas of Gotthold Ephraim Lessing in the drama *Nathan der Weise* (1779). In Wergeland's texts we see that Jews, the Catholic and Protestant Christians, and the Muslims really worship the same God, but in their own ways. Just as the sun's rays are reflected differently in sapphire, emerald, and ruby, so the light of divinity shines variously in people of diverse faiths, but it is the same light. The Jewess in "The Women in the Churchyard" explains this as she holds up a piece of jewelery containing worked stones:

Can you see? How clear all shine
each with the color of their mine
gives the heavenly image back.

Wergeland's Jewish poems were created in Norway in a certain historical situation; but as is customary in Wergeland, the perspective is universal and founded on a view of unity in creation, the human world, and history. The view opens out to the universal with validity for all ages. This is why the poems are felt to be at least as topical today as when they were written. Naturally, the persecution of the Jews during the Second World War has also helped to maintain their relevance. When Elie Wiesel was awarded the Nobel Peace Prize in 1986, he warned against indifference as one of the most perilous enemies of humanity. One could almost think he was familiar with "The Thistledown Gatherer" by Henrik Wergeland. In that poem indifference was pictured as a wingless angel with dead eyes and a complacent smile:

One angel only has stayed faithful to man:
the wingless one of Indifference
with dead eyes, fat cheeks and complacent smile

represents that in man which makes him distance himself from the suffering in the world. Wergeland's hero, and doubtless Wiesel's as well, is the small boy with the big heart who puts all his energies into doing what his conscience tells him is right, even if the tasks seem impossible.

Henrik Wergeland died on the night of July 12, 1845. He was thirty-seven years old. Thousands of people from all classes of society attended his funeral. But it was left to Jews from outside the boundaries of Norway to erect the first monument in his honor. It was placed on his grave in 1849. On its front was engraved: "Henrik Wergeland, the indefatigable advocate of freedom and justice for humanity and all citizens." During the German occupation of Norway in 1940–45 the Nazis kept a watch over Wergeland's grave on May 17 and other memorial days to prevent wreath-laying. The celebration of May 17 in the capital of Norway, Oslo, starts beside Henrik Wergeland's grave, where first schoolchildren and later young Jews pay tribute to his memory.

Dagne Groven Myhren
Assistant Professor of Nordic Literature,
University of Oslo

Chronology

1808	Henrik Wergeland is born at Kristiansand June 17
1811	Norway's first university founded
1814	The constitution of the Kingdom of Norway adopted May 17
1817	The family moves to Eidsvoll, where Henrik's father is appointed to the living
1825	Henrik Wergeland passes the university entrance examination in Kristiania
1829	Takes degree in theology
1830	*Creation, Man and Messiah*, a cosmological poem, published July 6
1831	Travels to England and France. Henrik Wergeland meets Moroccan Jews
1834–36	Studies medicine, does not take the examination
1839	Offer of a loan from King Carl Johan's personal funds, February/March, used for work on popular education. Henrik Wergeland marries Amalie Sophie Bekkevold at Eidsvoll April 27. "Proposal for the abolition of §2 of the Constitution, final passage," June 28
1840	Appointed director of the National Archives, which he founded
1841	"A Contribution to the Jewish Cause"
1841–43	*The History of the Constitution of Norway*
1842	*The Jew*, March 31. His proposal for an alteration to the constitution has a clear majority in the Norwegian parliament September 9. It is promising, but not sufficient to produce a change in the constitution. "The Jewish Cause in the Norwegian Parliament, propounded by Henrik Wergeland," October 26

1844   Henrik Wergeland is struck down by serious illness in May. *The Jewess*, published October 19. *Creation, Man and Messiah* is reworked and entitled *Man*—published January 1845

1845   Henrik Wergeland dies at Kristiania on the night of July 12 and is buried in the churchyard of Our Saviour July 17. The memoir entitled *Hazelnuts* is published posthumously July 20

1849   A monument to the Jewish people unveiled at Henrik Wergeland's grave on June 17

1851   Clause 2 of the constitution of Norway rescinded and Jews granted free access to Norway

The Army of Truth

The Army of Truth

Words? Those sounds the world despises.
    Words in poems?
Even more to be disdained!
Ah, how feeble are your powers
    to defend
all the truth that man denies!

Thunder crack and lightning flash
    at its presence!
Hosts of angels should come swooping
down from heaven to the rescue
    far and wide
spread the knowledge of its glory.

Oh, why can it not come winging
    from on high?
Truth, that with a starry birth
wears a helmet brightly gleaming
    wielding swords
fiercely sharp instead of feathers.

Oh, why then does it not pitch camp
    tent on tent
white on every mountainside?
Oh, why then are not its heroes
    strongly ranged
to keep mastery over life?

The fort of darkness is well guarded.
    Superstition
rests secure on stony columns.
Numerous as Egypt's serpents
    round truth's temple
range the black-clad guards of error.

Forward, though, you feeble lines!
    Words are armies!
On this earth your victory
was promised by the Lord, Light's father,
    when you serve
Truth itself, his child, alone.

Onward, words, you sons of truth!
    En avant!
In the end the hearts of men
will be your victorious home.
    Then your light
will with courage bear them on.

Forward, with your boldest faces
    Words of truth!
For the greatest power on Earth
has been granted you by God:
    Because never
Could you die in Truth's pure mouth!

Courage take then, all you small ones!
    Truth's great cause
Only triumphs in defeat.
Storm the bitter heights of lies!
    Raze them to the ground with Truth!

Originally translated by G. M. Gathorne-Hardy.

The Three

What beautiful temples of human love are the public inns of the Orientals! Turks and Bukhars have their caravanseries, the Persians their khans, the Hindus their resting places like sacred edifices, the Bedouins and the wild Kabyles their inviolable marabouts, and all are welcome to the Arab's tent, without discrimination. If he had been rich and not camped all over the desert, he too would have built caravanseries and khans for the stranger, for those are only an exalted transformation of his father's tents. It was the same hospitality of the tent which led to the building of the stone halls where the traveling Turk stables his horse and rests at ease, where the Armenian can leave his camel, where the Jew or the Nazarene has room for his bundle and himself in the ever-open hospitable cells.

Every religion has a gentle and loving heart. These hospitable institutions were provided by the faith which we Christians believe to have the hardest heart. They are religious in their origins, whether they have been created at public or private expense. It is often the latter. The pious Mohammedan or Hindu makes a legacy to these hostels as the Christian does to churches, convents, and hospitals. He wishes to help *the whole of humankind* when he builds an inn with gates open to the four corners of the world, or sinks a well in the desert, or directs a fountain to the animals' resting place. He gives thought to them as well, the old, gruff, bearded philanthropist. May Allah, Brahma, and the God of the Christians bless him!

Somewhere beyond the Dead Sea in sun-scorched Syria there is a desert, which the mercy of the infidels has left alone—not that it has not been discovered, but because Allah has given here, at the close of the day's journeying, a natural caravansery in the shape of a gigantic plane tree with space, shelter, and fresh water for a whole caravan if need be. Chance brought together here one evening a Mohammedan, a Christian, and a Jew. The Mohammedan, a mullah or priest, had scarcely watered his horse before a black dot on the horizon announced a stranger's arrival. This was the Christian, a monk of the Order of the Holy Mount. A mule was carrying him from Haleb to Jerusalem. "Salem aleikum!" said the mullah to the Nazarene, who returned his greeting in God's name. The stars were already bright and the howl of the jackals loud when the Jew, a rabbi from Damascus, unnoticed— for he came on foot—stepped onto the small plot of grass engendered by the fountain under the plane tree. In the days of King Solomon the fountain had also fostered this tree, and now as a good foster son's return, it supported its foster mother with shade. Like mothers in their old age the maternal spring was still singing her lullaby. To this murmur the three travelers, after friendly converse, fell asleep at last, each in his root hollow of the huge tree, and to the same murmur they woke up at dawn.

The desert lay beneath the mist within its horizon like a vast violet-blue ocean surrounded by mountains covered with the wonderful roses of Damascus. At one point in the east, angels seemed to be busy putting up golden spears as for a tent. The travelers could see that the sun was on the verge of rising. Something moved their hearts, their lips trembled. Each of them wished to greet God in his own way, but alas!—each was afraid of hurting the feelings of the other two. During their talk the previous evening they had learned to respect each other; but now—how could the mullah worship Allah aloud without disturbing the devotions of the Nazarene and the Jew, and the others felt likewise. Yet still the urge to give vent to their feelings at this supreme moment, and to thank the Highest for his protection in this paradisal shelter, was so great in them that their lips trembled. But still, none spoke. Quietly and hesitantly the Mohammedan saddled his horse, but without making much progress. The monk was equally slow with his mule, the rabbi tied his bundle and untied it again. They were men with tact and sympathy for each other and respect for other beliefs. Already thousands of glittering lances gleamed over the top of the rosy mountain. At the next moment the glorious image of the most High would appear, and must the worshipers remain silent? They longed to speak, but no prayer, no hymn of praise was uttered.

Then, at the same moment, from the same branch of the plane tree
a bullfinch, a wagtail, and a thrush tuned up their morning song. The
clear trill of the bullfinch blended with the warbling of the other birds
in a sublime, jubilant chorus.

"Why do we wait, brothers?" they all exclaimed. "Yes, with what
we long to say?" asked the mullah, bending three times to the earth.
"With the praise of Jehovah, the Highest," said the rabbi, folding his
hands across his breast. "Yes," said the Christian priest, making the
sign of the cross, "is this not a sign from Heaven that our praise too
will be pleasing to the Lord, although we express it differently?"And
suddenly, like the birds overhead, all three with a friendly glance at
each other, each in his way burst into a song of praise to the Creator
of themselves and of all things.

The mullah sang:
Allah, Allah, great and good!
Evermore be Allah praised!
See his word in floods of light
streaming from his paradise.
See the Prophet's great commandment:
"Worship Allah, love thy neighbor!"
over all the heavens spreading,
carried on the rays and shining
clear on every twig and leaf.

See, the distant palm is lit
like a Kaaba's vaulted dome!
    The very grass
turns adoring to the East;
and the fig leaf's modest hands
bathed in baptism of dew
are lifted up as if they would
blend their humble, silent prayers
with Life's echoing cries of Joy;
Allah, Allah, evermore
be praise and glory without end
to Him who searches for the worm
Underneath the ferny chill

with His warm benevolence,
to give comfort to its need!
    He who spreads
above the head of Earth's proud lord
and his momentary dust
the radiant arms of His affection.
Allah! Allah! To Him be praise!
    The rabbi sang:
Now all glory to Jehovah!
Merciful his sternest judgment.
How the mountainous clouds tremble!
Seraphs hover in the East . . .
See now how they spread their wings,
moving ever closer, closer
with loud cries of Hallelujah.

The gates of Eden open wide.
    Cherubim,
Zadikim all crowned with palms
wait aloft to catch the sigh
they can hear from Israel.
Mourning songs they glorify
with a choir of joyful hymns
    which they bear
in triumph to the ear of Grace,
show to those bent down with sorrow
    victory's palms
over the high throne of rest.
Hallelujah! In the east
mercy's rosary shines through:
sparkling Cherubim like beads
leap above the mountain tops.
High above a Zion rises
wreathed with cerulean rays.
Gilded temple columns up there
tower like Solomon's great temple.

. . . Look how purple velvet glows
   deep within!
   Golden red
seven-armed candelabrum glimmers
like a constellation from
a duskiness of deeper crimson
rising from the sea of darkness.
   In the heavens
David's harps seem strung for music.
Notes are struck from golden strings
sounding from the morning clouds.
And on either side are blazing
all along the horizon line
where lie the tents of Israel's tribes
behind the sunrise and its rays.
There Juda the blessed camps
with the right of the mighty,
the pearly rows of Ruben's tents,
Levi's towers, Asser, Gad,
Sebulon mongst shady palms,
Isaschar and Ephraim,
Simeon and Benjamin,
liberated Nephtali,
Dan, Manasse—they inhabit
the rosy Canaan of the dawn.

Glory be to great Jehovah!
Now the morning of his judgment
means their night will soon have passed.
   To the faithful
our Messiah shall come again
radiant from heaven above.
   And the Christian, the Nazarene, sang:
Praise be to Almighty God!
See the morning light beginning
to proclaim his name abroad.

Look how the tufted clumps of grass
bend to worship Him who grants it,
refreshing dew as his blessing.
For its pure and holy moisture
sprinkled over grass and branches
sanctifies both grove and meadow
as a sacred temple hanging
where the blessed ones can worship.

Every sunlit stem that sparkles,
moves in waves across the plain,
is a staff supporting Faith;
every leaf's a winged angel,
every twig a cross of gold,
so the air is richly filled.
Every flower the sun has gilded
is a cup brimful of mercy.
Heavenly Love has tenderly
granted it His heart's whole bounty,
    passed the chalice, overflowing
    to each pure soul
    who is aware
of the ascension here renewed
daily from the morning clouds—
to the promise that is written
on the meadow white with dew
of a Love all-merciful
shining out in gentle rays,
flowing from the brimming cups
down upon the whole of Earth—
    of an Eden
entrusted by the God of Mercy,
ringed around by rosy daybreaks
    in whose clouds
saints in angels' strong embrace
with unfettered arms are praising
the name of the Unnameable.

This was the message that came simultaneously from the hearts of these believers. Then they shook hands and set out happily along their various routes through the desert: the mullah journeyed toward Baghdad, the monk toward Jerusalem, the rabbi toward Damascus. But when they had gone a short distance, it seemed as if the same thought occurred to them and made them send a glance of gratitude to the hospitable plane tree, now far away like a St. Helena in the ocean of air. That thought came to all three: What if the birds who taught us to worship in truth, were three angels flown down from Heaven because they took pity on our frailty?

Originally translated by I. Grøndahl.

Christmas Eve

Who can't remember
A storm far worse than any Heaven can send?
A storm as if each soul from Cain's to the one
    God last condemned,
for cursing Earth, might have escaped from Hell,
and tempted them to turn their back on Heaven?

A storm, the terrors
of whose dreaded voice can't be forgotten.
For all had thought: it must be sent
    for *my* fault only;
the tempest's thunder must mean only mine,
my sin has been reported to the Lord.

A storm whose strength
can teach priest and believers to conjure up
demons in the element whose roar
    the old can hear
from childhood onward even into deafness . . .
an earthquake of the clouds, air's judgment day?

A storm that shook
the strong heart in its shelter in the breast,
a storm from Heaven calling his own name
    to stern account
by spirits that the gale led on before him,
while every treetop shouted like a raven.

But raven hid itself
deep in the cliff-side, wolf controlled his hunger,
and fox, cowering, dared not venture out.
    Inside the house
every light dimmed, the watchdog was let in . . .
In such a storm prayers rise up to our God!

〜

In such a storm—it was on Christmas Eve—
when day turned into night before its time,
an aged Jew was making his way homeward,
through Sweden's wilderness, the Tived forest.
The village on this side awaited him,
come from those on the other just for Christmas,
the young girls with impatience, for in his rucksack
he carried ribbons, brooches, all they needed
for Christmas Day, the next ones and the New Year.
They waited in suspense but not in fear;
Because "Old Jacob" had never let them down
on any Christmas: for he came as surely
as Christmas Eve itself.

In such a storm . . .

"Hush! Is it coming back,
the gale that bellowed through the trees?
It screamed, and now it comes again."
Old Jacob stops, and listens.
Now all is quiet. But then the gale increases,
to crash like a waterfall on someone drowning.
He soldiers on. "Hush! There it sounds again!"
A din that rises over the forest's roar.
"The false owl shrieks just like a little child.
Who would allow a child out in such weather?
The wolf would take more care of her offspring!"

The old man trudges on through the snow,
but then it cries again, without a doubt;
for from far off this whirlwind builds a tower
of circling snow that covers all the forest,
and sweeps a *word*, a single word along;
at once he turns toward the place it came from,
working his way deeper into the woodland
and deeper in the snow and in the night
that like a coal-black mountain wall rears up
against his every step, dim lit by flakes,
as if the whole white forest were a crowd
of flying, whirling, veiled ghosts and spirits,
who howled and barred his way at every moment,
airily spinning, growing fearfully,
and vanished then among the threatening tree trunks.

Still the old man fights on against the tempest,
prevailing when it waxes; when it wanes,
drawing its breath, he listens on his knees.
But soon leaps up and challenges the darkness,
as when a dwarf digs through the pitch-black soil.
He hears nothing more. The old man trembles,
he fears evil spirits are tricking him,
and mumbles out the well-known prayers for help.
Then the sobbing sounds again, this time much closer;
his own voice is blown back by the gale
to shelter in his mouth. But there, yes, there!
Ten paces more! Where something dark is moving
upon the snow, as if the gale were playing
with a tree stump dislodged at the root.

"O Jehovah! An arm! O Jehovah!
A child, a child! But oh, it is dead!"
Ah, did the shining stars on this dark night
when the star of Bethlehem shone among them,
think that no good is ever done on Earth?

For not one of them saw that this Old Jacob,
as glad as if he'd come upon a treasure,
straightway threw down all his wealth, his bulging pack;
pulled off his threadbare coat and wrapped it round
the lost child's limbs, then bared his breast
and laid the ice-cold cheek closely against it,
until his heartbeat woke her. Then up he leaped.
But now where should he go? The storm
had quite covered his tracks. Yet he did not fear.
For in the thundering of the wind-torn treetops
he only heard the jubilant harps of David;
he saw the flying drifts of snow as cherubs,
who, borne on swan-white wings, pointed the way;
and on the haphazard, winding path he took
he felt the strong pull of the Lord's own hand.

But how to find a house in wild Tived
on such a night, when no one dared a light?
Halfway across he knew was but one dwelling,
whose low roof could not be distinguished from
the snow, nor its black wall from the bare rock.
But brought by a miracle he came up against it.
There he sank down; his strength was all but gone.
And many a cloud of snow flew till he could
drag himself and burden to the door.
Then he knocked softly, for the child was sleeping,
and only then thought of his missing pack
which meant he carried nothing at all to offer
the good poor folk who would soon now come running
to fling open the door with kindly haste.
Alas, how long he waited till they answered:
"In Jesu's name, who knocks on such a night?"
"It is Old Jacob. Can you not hear me?"
"Jacob, the old Jew?"
"*Jew?*" sounded in terror
a man's voice and a woman's.
"Then stay outside. We have nothing to pay with.

You'd only bring misfortune to our house,
this night, the one when *Him* you slew was born!"
"I?"
"Ay, your people and that is the sin
through thousand generations must be punished."
"Alas, for on this night the shivering dog's let in!"
"Yes, the dog,
but no Jew into a Christian house."

He heard no more. Those hard and cruel words
cut through him keener than the winter wind,
and, stronger than the wind, they threw him down,
down in the snow, bent over the sleeping child.
Then, as he turned to look toward the window,
his gaze expecting that the white face might
appear again, it seemed as though he sank
in feathers, and a blissful warmth flowed through
his veins, and that familiar beings, whispering,
sounded like harp's notes in the summer breeze
and flew about his couch, till one of them
said, raising a warning finger: "Come! He sleeps!"
And into a bright-lit hall nearby
they disappeared; only the child remained,
drawing his covers warmly closer round him,
until it seemed to him he fell asleep.
It was the snow, falling as a soft shroud.

"Oh, Jesus, see the Jew who sits there still!"
the man cried, looking out onto the morning.
"Chase him away then! It is Christmas Day!"
chimed in his wife. "Look at the greedy Jew,
how tight he holds his bundle to his breast!
All he thinks about is gaining riches,
staring in at the window with fixed gaze,
as if *we* had any coins to spare."
"We might as well see what he has got, though . . ."
"All right, Jew, let us see!"

    The pair went out.
Then saw the frozen stare in the dead eyes.
They turned more pale than he, called out in fear
and trembled with remorse. "O Lord! O Lord!
Oh, what a terrible misfortune! Lift him up,
the bundle too." Then they loosed his coat,
to see, with arms locked round the old Jew's neck,
Margretha, their own child, a corpse like him.
No lightning strikes so sharp, no snake so swiftly
as pain and horror rammed that couple's hearts.
The snow was no whit whiter than the father,
the gale wailed no louder than the mother.
"Oh, God has punished us! Not the fierce storm,
but our own cruelty has killed our child!
In vain, alas!—as he knocked on our door—
we too shall knock upon the door of Mercy."

        ⌇

When the road through the forest was cleared of snow,
a man came from the farm where Gretha lived
as foster child, from whence, the Yule bells sounding
        sweetly,
before the storm set in she had been walking
to visit her parents on that Christmas Eve.
He did not come to ask about the child,
but for the Jew, from all the village girls,
whose hopes to go to church were now postponed
to New Year's Day—if he could be found.

But there he lay, a corpse before the fire.
His host, with gaze as frozen as the Jew's,
his body bent as crooked as the corpse,
sat staring stiffly into the red embers
and constantly stoked the blaze, so that the body
might be straightened out and the hands folded.
In front of them Margrethe's mother knelt,
folding the stiff arms of her little one

closer and closer round the dead man's neck.
"For she no more belongs to us," she sobbed,
"he has bought our child by his own death.
We dare not take our little Gretha from him,
for she must beg for us of our Lord Jesus
his intercession; to his father
the poor Jew will complain . . ."

Originally translated by I. Grøndahl.

On the Sick-Bed

These fiery stabs, this icy thrill
    that shudders through my breast:
Call them thy triumph, Death, they bring
to me the balmy breeze of spring
that stirs the heavens, now warm, now chill,
    the April of my rest.

But still my heart is fighting here
    against the spears of Death.
Beating as usual day by day
to keep the enemy at bay.
My mind is tranquil, bright and clear
    to heed my steady breath.

So then, perhaps, I yet may know
    my briar in all its bloom,
whose springing shoots at first were seven,
then grew to nine, and now eleven,
and others too, I trust, may grow,
    should Death delay his doom.

You flower as where in Gulistan
    the Persian roses stand!
Yet none your hidden plot will seek,
you blossom in the desert bleak,
where I was driven, a banished man,
    from kindred and from land.

Here to this barren loneliness
    driven by my country's ban,
by angry fools, who little guess
how glorious here the woods are grown
where I have lived, like cage-bird flown
    or the free Indian.

Brazil's deep spreading forest, where
    the lofty palm tree towers,
whose trunk the bright camellias twine,
mixed with the blue of passion flowers,
    is nowhere near so proud, so fair
as this lone haunt of mine.

Here visions gather, thick and fast,
    and spirits make their way,
like clouds hung low on treetop crowns
seeking their way through woodland scenes
where memories throng with times long past
    in solitude at last.

And yet, here in my dear retreat
    I have been taken ill
with sorcery or some snake bite,
my arm is weak, my cheek is white,
my pulse can only feebly beat,
    no energy I feel.

Ah! mighty Death's insisting will
    has broken my thread of life;
I long to be with those I know,
and tell them the right way to go
to see this garden blossoming still
    that I tended with my breath.

See! how the nectar trickles sweet
    from every budding rose.
Doesn't each open petal bear
a song of love that's written there?
Doesn't each blossom's purple heart
    a sacred book disclose?

If only Death would stay my fate
    till every rose were grown!
But all around I hear his feet
coming to claim me for his own,
And now his arrow swift he sends
    and soundless from his bow.

Ah, I am bathed in purity!
    I have forgiven all!
A finger lightly touched my brow,
An angel's. Mother's call,
A dewy flower my soul is now,
    new-born in sanctity.

Originally translated by G. M. Gathorne-Hardy.

Voice in the Wilderness

Hearts of Christians all should glow
with the warmth of Christmas fare,
    Honey-sweet,
heaped for a whole world in need,
should it chance to enter there;
decked with sprigs of roses gay,
as for festive holiday.
    Woe! Woe!
Ice they are, or lumps of snow,
stones, within whose crannies dwell
swarms obscene from blackest hell;
All their softness merely mold,
though like velvet to behold.

Now, a clear transparent sheen
should on every brow be seen,
like that radiance milky-white
where a star would pierce the night.
Gentle smiles on every face,
eloquent, with kindness blest,
as if all the human race
were its loved and welcome guest.
    Woe! Woe!
Reckoning tablets dark and drear
hide those noble aspects now,
    to and from
ciphered over either brow;
and hot tears of maudlin passion,
and the manic leer of vice,

—features all in savage fashion
        bruised and ravaged—
the nation's face have sorely damaged.

Quenched, the fire of love departs,
as the color from the rose,
and the people shut their hearts
like a miser's coffer close;
while a cold estranging mind
severs each man from his kind,
as when some poor wanderer tramps
through the city streets alone,
where in every pane the lamps
are extinguished one by one.
"Give me shelter!" he will plead.
        Who will heed?
Shake, that is the wisest plan,
from your feet, the dust, O man!
Shun this town, and seek the lee
of some friendlier forest tree.
Turks and savages possess
more fraternal kindliness
and humanity than we.

As with him who wandered lonely
through the waste, deserted town,
haunted by the echoes only
from the trodden pavement thrown,
such is the poet's hapless fate
who receives in trust from heaven
oil for empty vessels given,
and that charge does not forsake
in trifling for the world's delight.
But still strikes in lyric chords
harmonies to God's own words,
proclaims the solemn call of right
where to duties long foregone

errant hearts are barred with stone.
    Woe! Woe!
Once we all of us did swear
troth beneath God's roof, to wear
crowns of innocence that day,
crowns which in a year decay;
women round their heads have wreathed
garlands fresh of roses white
where the purple scarce has breathed;
men, that day, in open sight—
although perhaps with less display—
wore at least a little spray.
But the promise that they gave,
    full persuaded,
and in accents clear and deep,
    was to keep
and to carry to the grave,
hearts untainted and unfaded
as those flowers the day they trod
in the presence of their God.

O, and then, with sinless sight
you glimpsed God, and how he spanned
utmost depth and farthest height.
How the unnamed insect flew,
to the same encircling hand,
fluttered, turned itself or crept
as the proudest stars that swept
within the arms of endless view.
And you felt you too might nurse
in your arms the universe,
earth and heavenly spheres combined,
that an equal bliss you knew
while you to your warm hearts drew
as your fellows all mankind.

Originally translated by G. M. Gathorne-Hardy.

The Maple and the Pine

THE PINE

What is this song I hear at dusk
    come gaily from your crown?
And rouses all my somber boughs
    to feel its joyful sound?

THE MAPLE

It is a merry swarm of bees
    I've given shelter here,
and since they came the forest owns
    no tree of happier cheer.

They play their music all day long
    and all I pay for this
is leave to take some honey from
    the surplus of my leaves.

Each branch is filled with busyness
    and every little leaf
where lazy caterpillars crawled
    is food for industry.

Honey and wax are stored inside
    the woodpecker's old nest.
I feel the heart within my breast
    with love is truly blest.

THE PINE
Aha! So you let alien tribes
       your riches sweet to steal?
I would prefer that my new shoots
       should fall before the gale.

And all my golden pollen I
       would fling to wind and weather
before I'd let such trespassers
       rob me of my treasure.

Like molten silver on the rock
       my turpentine runs free,
as it has done a hundred years
       and will eternally.

THE MAPLE
Permit the bee, a cake of wax
       he'll make for you again.

THE PINE
What's honey and wax? a century
       I've lived without their gain.

I represent my native land,
       the knowledge of that task
is all I need, to others I
       pay no heed if they ask.

THE MAPLE
Then drive away all active life
       and joy of life as well,
And stay a century more where none
       but wretched beggars dwell.

The dish love gives is free to all
    though with no pomp and pride
it pays again and yet again
    with coin of gratitude.

Give sap and honey gives again,
    shelter, and music sounds,
Give freedom, somber pine, and get
    the life you see I found.

Then listen to the merriment
    in that old maple tree!
He has like me, the little thing,
    some hospitality.

That swarm of bees so hard at work
    round about his crown
is busy heaping riches up
    to sweeten folks in town.

The willow and the rowan too!
    Look round you, clever pine!
For all about you, can't you see,
    noble examples shine.

THE PINE
But doesn't idleness taste sweet?
    You really must allow
that solitude's a blessed state,
    and I'm not changing now!

Originally translated by G. M. Gathorne-Hardy.

Follow the Call

Royal eagle, chained and bound
by the leg, with broken wing,
who for over twenty years—
since the shot that crippled him—
has served as a fettered guard
in a poor smallholder's yard.
Despite his wounded limb he has
less of sadness than the poet
born into a wilderness
unheeding as this dreary land.
     With a voice
that never travels further than
the unheard breath upon his lips.

He is like a muffled bell
covered with a deadening cloth,
or a rose bush that is hid
in the shade beneath a bush.
To spread wide his longing wings
let his voice go flying free,
like those happy ones who sing
to the eager crowds of hearers
is impossible for one
bound with the bands of a minor tongue.

Rather be an Indian
native-born and free to roam,
belong to a tribe in tropic climes,
or be an Araucanian,

for they would think the poet holy,
bid him to join their festivals,
build him a shelter out of palm leaves,
sit around his fire and listen
carefully to all his songs,
     learn word for word
to sing in chorus the refrain,
voice his works with might and main.
When he dies his audience
will gather every word he gave them
     so coming singers
will in time again perform them.

Other light than that which shines
forth from out the poet's lay
is not seen by those poor hearers;
     vices, virtues,
wandering by separate ways
home to immortality,
and the judgment of the Lord
the poet knew before and taught
his people of Him through his song.
     The very thought
of the Spirit they adore
is carried to them by the vision
they have barely glimpsed before.
Like the pearls which shimmering through
the waves that billow far above
amidst the wildness of their chanting
speak of glowing revelation.

Ah, but we ourselves are still
savages in mind and will,
sometimes even in our customs.
The Indians of the far West
who in their tribes live far apart,
when they meet are not so brutal

though they drink each other's blood,
as in many-sected Europe
where hatred rules so bitterly.

But our world must still be young,
Sagas of each race must be
still merely its cradlesong
and its childhood fairy tale.
Creatures from the age of Chaos,
Megasaurs from Amazon,
Leviathan who swallowed Jonah,
and monstrous serpents, still survive.
Deserts that spread a thousand miles,
        a thousand wide,
thundering with lions' roar
mock our busy human ways.
The mountain, that in Noah's time
        stood supreme
raising proud its pointed summits,
showing not the slightest sign
of its shoulders crumbling down
to create a fruitful field.
But see its formidable faces
glittering like icy crystals
where the precipice falls steepest,
violet and heavenly blue!
What has smoothed that horn of alp,
polished brightly its hard flank
speck by speck and grain by grain?
        Drops of rain,
the gentle touch of softest breath
on atom-woven cloaks of cloud,
like feathers on a misty hat.
What has crushed granite to sand
and flushed out the ruddy spar,
so it heaps up at the foot
more and more a pristine white?

The gentle cycles of the water,
this measured pacing of the ocean,
and the calm beat of the waves,
in its deep and constant motion
seems the breathing of a world.
And for a millennium
every year in summertime
the moss puts forth its little flowers
shaped like tiny silver goblets
covering the bare gray rocks,
where among the scattered flora
lofty spruces find their feet.

~

There is nothing, great or small,
that is fruitless, or decayed,
but its ending keeps a purpose,
however hidden that may be.
        The meadow dew,
Melting in the sun's kind warmth,
is gathered into depths of cloud
as a delicate hovering veil
woven out of flower tints;
and the gauzy parachutes
spun by ancient willow trees,
industriously as the mother
weaving warmth against the winter,
are not stolen by the breeze,
but when they fall to earth are taken
by the ants to build their nest.

Must the poet's word, the pure
dew from sparks of light, as warm
as the blood coursing in his breast,
be the only vital thing
in this world that vanishes
from memory without a trace?

Come now! if our Lord's own voice
fills your heart with tempest's power
in the desert loud proclaim it!
And from darkness your strong voice
will call the dawn of better days.
Come now! let your fingertips
caress the harp strings so their tones
send a glow into the gloom!

Then from among that distant people
terrified and lost in silence,
a few may yet, like Laps from over
the stony billows of the mountains,
when a vision of distant flames
calls them from their huts of mud,
hurry there where the minstrel tunes
his harp to sound the truest tones;
then when he comes to raise his eyes,
he'll see the modest group around him.

That is enough!
He will know that all his needs
do not crave a million souls,
but two or three stand firm together.

Originally translated by G. M. Gathorne-Hardy.

Wanton Weeds

"Now, farewell!" said my friend one summer evening when we had
gone out for some air after one of our frequent discussions on the
coming of the Jews to Norway. "This will have to be the last time!
But, Brother, what kind of a flower bed have you got here? Nothing
but weeds except for that sunflower! Thistle, poppy, toadflax, burdock,
great mullein *and* henbane, for heaven's sake. Though something
could probably be made of that plot, just as it could of Norway, if
you just cleared away all those stones. It's a little Norway, neglected
and full of weeds."

My friend's objections to the Jews annoyed me so much that I
could not fall asleep. So I went downstairs and outside, where I sat
on the ground. It was approaching dawn in the month of June. But
what should I see and hear! As the first red line ran along the hilltops
I heard a sound close by like a faint clapping of hands and I saw the
sunflower opening its manifold ear-shaped petals and seeming of its
own accord to turn them this way and that to listen. But its aim
was to wake the plants sleeping around it on the rocky slope; for
immediately there sounded, in a voice like a kind of Jew's harp,

THE SUNFLOWER
Well, I never! It's two o'clock;
Everyone is still fast asleep.
But if I'm not too much mistaken
through narrowed eyes what do I see
in the garden all around me
but a wide-awake morning dame strutting about.

That's right! Goodmorrow, *Marigold*, my dame!
Here where I stand in my cursed place,

since my master drew from out of his pocket
just *my* little seed, which he then set down
in this place where I could not avoid being with
the very worst company—just look here,
while I have watched since the mountain crests
glowed with the first pale rose-red sheen,
these wretches around me soundly slept!
Poppy, wake up, you sleepy Hound!
Toadflax, make use of your gaping Mouth!
Mullein, leave off
your nodding!
Henbane, you troll,
drunk since last night
dazed with the liquor
mixed with the poison,
that you know well
how to suck out of the stoniest cracks—
away with a drop from your cup,
Burdock, lurking hunter!
Thistle, hey! Just you give the white
Campion a nudge in the side!
Wake up each other, then you will see
enacted in play a satiric idea.
This moment's our time.
You know that it's brief:
Only from daybreak on the hilltop
until the first ray of sunlight breaks out.
Then quickly get started!
But—confounded misfortune!
Isn't that our Master sitting there?
He'll tear me up by all my roots
if he's heard my ingratitude,
my moaning over how I've come
to be here (where at least I'm ruler)
to make my entrance out of the earth,
when otherwise it is true enough
that I'd have died off in his pocket.

Quiet! Here we must be crafty.
Bindweed, just you sneak over there!
His pipe is lying on his knee,
so I'm pretty sure he's dozing.
Just to test him, give him, *Mullein,*
a little tap upon the back
of his hand's soft level surface
with your gray flannel leaves!
. . . Ah! He can surely stand a rap,
so I can dare to mount my play.

Do you see all these my hundred
ears, all so finely gilded,
always filled with the latest news
that they've snapped up here and there?
For example, just last evening
I picked up with them in amazement,
the hours and hours of conversation
of our master and his friend
until both of them were utterly spent,
and parted with a weary farewell.

But what can never be forgotten
is that this friend, the bitter, bad one
came to resemble this rocky slope,
as may be some wild vegetation
may have spread itself there too
in his country and his nation.

Now! For us it well may be
the greatest honor.
So therefore let us imitate
what I heard then may quite well happen
in Norway, the land of freedom!
We'll create a little Norway
here from one end of our slope
to its other infertile edge!

Now each one must singly choose
a faith, or a denomination!
And then apply to me, who'll play
the ruling Lutheran national church,
for a place within our land!
Whatever madness may be blended
with the belief he represents
can have no influence on his rights.
But should the supplicant be a Jew
we shall at once repudiate him.
Now choose! And only leave behind
Judaism and scorn
for the mignonette down there,
that for so long
has tried to make its way out here
seeking shelter from the sun's heat!
Let it fade there on the slope!
Should I then lend it my shade?
Nay, it is as it's always been,
the thorn in my eye.

Now there was an uproar and a jostling. "I am a Roman Catholic,"
said the *Mullein*, "because I resemble the Strasborg-Münster." "And
I am Greek," said the *Rose Bay Willow Herb.* "Come along, take
your place," nodded the *Sunflower* graciously. "Our Norway is a free
country as you see." "And it's true that I'm no more a Christian than
a Jew; although I do have a Christian name; I am a Quaker," said the
brown *Dock.* "Never mind about the name. Take your place!" replied
the *Sunflower.* "But I," mumbled the *Poppy,* "I suppose I'll be excluded,
because I am a Muslim?" "Far from it! You're welcome!" "Then
perhaps I can be a fire worshiper?" said the fiery yellow *Crowfoot.*
"And I cultivate sun, moon and stars?" said the *Thistle.* "And I
Juggernaut?" "And I the great serpent?" "And I the cow?" "But we
worship idols," shouted a whole clump of weeds. "Doesn't matter,"
said the *Sunflower,* "The borders aren't closed to you." "But to me,"
mumbled the wan *Henbane,* "I am a Jezide; I cultivate the Devil, the
principle of evil." The *Sunflower* pricked up a couple of its ears and
rubbed them together as grasshoppers do with their wings; but after

a moment's consideration it said: "The law allows you to stay in this country as well. You are welcome, Devil worshiper!"

Then the *Sunflower* bent down a little and said in a severe voice:
But you, small plant, that modestly
tries to creep from off the heath
beneath the shadow of our leaves
to flourish in a richer soil,
tell me: I think from your bearing
and your creeping you are a Jew?

THE MIGNONETTE
How definite it's come to be.
My confession sounds quite humble:
God is Father to one and all.

THE SUNFLOWER
In our wise law there are written
words that with eternal curse
refuse your right to breathe our air.
The people's will firmly demands
That you are to be evicted
From a free enlightened land.

But I interrupted it with a good nap, so that put an end to the ruling church; and when I had got rid of the weeds, I discovered to my joy both a little Rosa Centifolia that I had planted in the spring but given up hope for, and one of the beautiful three-colored convolvulus with red, white, and blue flowers, climbing prettily around the rose bush. That had been somewhat stunted, of course, yet it sported a well-formed bud, and with that sweet mouth I heard it say to the Mignonette:

"Come to us, you banished one! We will protect you. We are Norway's rightful symbols: We are *Love* and *Liberty*."

Prose translated by Anne Born;
poetry originally translated by G. M. Gathorne-Hardy.

Briar Shoots

Briar shoots, briar shoots.
Briar shoots that carry blossoms . . .
Virtues, loveliest shown in troubles,
Woes that never cease from hoping,
Faith, that God when burdened held to,
blameless neck so cruelly bowed.

    O the women of Judea
      beauteous roses sprung of old!
Tender mothers walk with heroines,
Pious Ruth, the Maccabean,
Miriam's honor, streaming honey,
    Judith's rose with reddened thorn.
O I hear, I see before me
    Judea's women, at their door
in the evening deftly spinning
sing to the zither with sweet voices
round them children toddling gaily,
    growing daughters early veiled.

Judea's valleys are deserted
all the roses are destroyed,
roots wide scattered; but I see
now the creeping twigs are shooting.
Judea's roses in full flower:
    women's grace in sorrow's splendor.
Maternal care and Faith that's burning,
    Loyal wife in hardship cheerful,

openhanded to the needy,
ably tending to the household—
these roses while the world continues
    grow on the disperséd briars.

Alas! and these our sister-branches,
    rounded just as Eve's sweet bosom,
forced to crawl along cold stones,
or to bloom alone and sadly,
roses languish behind curtains
    in the twilight window frame.

What if Norway's fair green valleys
offered them a home to live in?
What if now and then its cool blood
Mixed became with Oriental?
Then will only Love hold sway,
not the roaring Lion of Law.

Translated by Anne Born.

The Jewess

Doff your veil, O Jewess! Doff it,
Rachel, O thou wondrous beauty!
Come, stand forth! And then, if need be,
kneel before these Nordic men,
who will give judgment on your people
more rigorous than Eli's ruling.

Now, away with arguments!
How can there be need of "for"?
What can be equal to "against"?
Both of them, both "pro" and "contra"
melt away before her eyes.

Oh, in them the light of Paradise
gleams with Oriental sunshine!
Yet how mild beneath them are
her long silken eyelashes
like soft undersides of palm leaves.
If they could be angered, they would
shoot a glance of glowing coal.
Now their gaze would cast a flare
like a splendid firework show,
with a fountain's lavish wealth
pour an endless radiant rain
formed of blue-black diamonds.

If the world should call you slave,
do not let your lips reply,

bare your forehead and it will lay
golden crowns at your feet.
Show your noble stature, and
queens will fall to their knees.

The radiant white of seraph wings
shines, fair Rachel, on your brow,
noble as Cornelia's,
thoughtful as the Blessed Mary's.
Yours alone a countenance
filled with purest dignity
of a priestess and a queen.
The unknown name of God must be
clearly written on your face.
The graceful curve of rose petals
seems to imitate your cheek,
and its delicate blush of color
is immortality's good health,
the rosy dawn of eternity
the scarlet light of cactus flowers,
bright alabaster all aglow.

The flowing waves of those long locks
are the apparel of Queen Eve
when she ruled supreme in Eden.
Their blackness seems as if the dust
of diamonds should cover them
and sparkling rays of starlight bathe them.
Those shining streams must emerge,
O thou wondrous beauty, from
the selfsame rich black source of flame
from where your eyes are beaming out;
for like those
glows their darkling mystery.
Rachel smiles. Gentle heaven!
Was it the purity of her soul,

the crown of pearl that is inherent
in the soul's pure raiment seen
starrily glinting at her lip?
Might just a little—in its bow—
of the white heart of a blessed one,
lifted on the wings of a smile,
appear in such ardent blood?

O my Jewess, you have conquered.
Human beings would take an oath
by their freedom; for you are
daughter of the centuries' thralldom,
and their tears of ignominy
have been blended with your mother's.

You won the victory without words,
by your own revelation.
In you the whole world shall conquer,
win back a true covenant
for a nobler and a more
paradisal tribe of Adam.

Come! Here Caucasians are blue,
Cedar-like the crowns of firs
sough above those of Lebanon.
The rounded earth is Canaan.
The handsomest of Nordic freemen
will dare to pay their court to you,
lead his bride into a valley
deeper and more beautiful
than Judea's under Carmel.

Should your bridal posy lack
the scarlet rose of Jericho,
the brilliant white of Sharon's lilies,
Rachel, think you not that Norway's

amethyst violets of springtime,
seraph-eyed convolvulus
would not well adorn your locks,
when they signify the tears
flowing out of true repentance?

Translated by Anne Born.

The Women at the Churchyard

Which is the word in every tongue
out of the cavalcades of words
where every wisdom-weighted thought
has a name by which it's known—
which concept in the soul's book,
bound up within the white bone,
among all its potentials
discovered or ascribed—
which idea that flies around
imagination's vast domain,
carefree as a butterfly,
so profound a peace could breathe,
so significant and silent,
so serene and calm, such peace,
as that word: a "churchyard."

There is peace and no more pain,
there is peace, but nothing else,
either contrary or blended,
while the very word "Peace,"
when it is uttered in our speech,
paints that other thought, of 'strife,"
inevitable and bloody, on
the wan gray mind-slate of the soul.
Inevitable in the idea,
thrown swiftly on the soul's bright mirror
as the rough breath of the wind
drums a figure in the snow,
paints for itself with every thought

the one that least deserves accusal.
Name but "Blessed" and "Accursed"
Straight it is written on the brow?
Name but "Love"—and what more
innocent word could be conceived?—
At once ideas quite contrary
("Jealousy," "Infidelity," "Hate"),
dance like witches all around it,
till, profaned and bereft,
the word has no more left of what
was heavenly, than a butterfly
that has lost its vital dust.
Name each peace-filled word, and see
what a doubting smile alights
on the eyes and lips of all
at the counterthought aroused!

But no mean thought can hold sway
for long against the word "Churchyard."
No concept that contradicts
the tranquillity it holds
has been dragged into the soul
beneath the crannies of the brain.
Among the words this hovers there:
starbright dove on soundless wings
is greeted joyously by mankind
who moves on earth and lives for heaven
and does reverence to those
who quietly tremble at the name.
There within the churchyard is
Heaven's forecourt, wherein each one—
Saint and Sinner, Good and Bad—
can lay down their heaviest burden,
the body formed of flesh and blood,
and hasten on along their way.
There the deadly pale-faced foes
rest in silence side by side,

until the boards crack, fall away,
the coffin crumbles, soil runs
and each with each blends their bones,
while their crosses up above
closely lean their tops together
beneath the weeping poplar boughs.
There the hate that goes on living
loses strength, is paralyzed
and can never follow further
than the heavy portal's locks:
through the black bars of the railings
peers the eye, the tears flow,
the casket silently sinks down,
the tears follow—and hate goes with them.

There, if two bitter enemies
should agonize in fire and flame,
sputtering with furious quarrel,
suddenly met there together
among the graves, with flowers bordered
on a narrow winding path:
hardly had they hurried past,
than they started, and then stopped,
cast their eyes down, saw a grave,
then raised their heads till eye met eye,
hand at once was clasped in hand
and they were reconciled until death.

But see, look round you at this fair
churchyard! Oh, how every grave
is an isle, whose groves of roses
and whose aster palms spring up
out of the quiet sea of grass,
like a merry zephyr moved
now and then by a small billow.
Here is an orchestra of songbirds,

soon as the last trace of snow
melts away along the avenue,
annually a favored spot
for their melodious festivals
that go on till winter comes.
No lofty church is standing here,
calling to mind the one true faith,
in this multitude of stones
raising up its conqueror's throne
to rule over the churchyard with,
high above
all who sleep beneath it, so
it cannot be what it was made for,
a resting place beneath the soil,
but by authority of the church,
allotted solely to its own members . . .

Here in this, the Lord's delightful
garden, consecrated to
devotions of a quiet mind,
sacred peace and fondest memories,
strolling down a poplar walk
two women friends go arm in arm.
The evening sky is passing fair;
with a pleasant serenade
the choir of birds accompanies them.

One of them, a Roman Catholic,
she who resembles eventide,
as she walks the whole time gazing
quietly, somberly, before her,
searches for a beauteous place
for her departed little one.
The other, given more to talking,
who seemingly is quite contented,
is a Protestant Lutheran.

Here, Rosalie, now this one says—
No place as this could be more lovely.
Here the twelve small white-clad girls
shall carry your dear little Anna.
And Rosalie, surely here,
with the aspen tree, just think!
Here Mother Nature has provided
a generous space to set a bench.
Here, when the shade of poplar's crown
throws its pyramidal coolness
we shall often sit, my friend,
when time's course shall reconcile
you to painful memories,
and listen to the aspen clapping
its castanets of leaves so softly
to the tunes of finch and whitethroat
about a swarm of evening midges
loath to let go of the day.
And when there's a little space
between the thorny boughs of roses
on the other side I'll get
a glimpse of that small narrow corner
which I, as a Protestant,
shall surely one day name as mine:
so from each our resting place
we shall go on after death
in some way to meet each other.
Memorials with marble brow,
they at least will see each other,
in the glimmering of moonlight.

ROSALIE (pointing at a woman sitting on a grave)
But Constance, goodness gracious me!
Do you not see the Jewess there?
This place should be saved for dogs
for it lies extremely close,
as you can see, to the corner

assigned to the synagogue,
so it ought to be enclosed
by itself with a high fence,
and no flowers should be placed
on its graves by any mourners.

But now, look at the Jewish corner!
This is dreadful, look at it,
it is a most lovely garden
full of all the fairest flowers,
crept in there from Christian graves?
And climbing plants running wild
have long since covered all the fence,
indeed make mock of law and order,
and leveled it down to the ground
by the sheer weight of sturdy stems.

CONSTANCE
Oh, my friend! You are quite right.
I found the place pleasant enough
but never noticed the disgusting
neighboring dwellers in earth's bosom.
Why, when Jack, my aging cat,
comes to the ending of his days,
I shall steal down here one evening
and bury him.

ROSALIE
So this place is not for us.

CONSTANCE
It seems not. But come along! You can
find another plot, I'm sure.

THE JEWESS (rising)
Ladies, dare I beg of you
here to make a little stay?

ROSALIE (making to leave)
The evening sun is dazzling us.

CONSTANCE
We are in a hurry.

JEWESS
Three minutes only. Two will do.

CONSTANCE
The Jewess bargains.

JEWESS
Look how the aspen stretches out
its shadow tent, where in its shade
you can find shelter from the sun.
For the words that will rob you of
only just the fewest minutes
we need precisely this sunny moment.
And if you will only permit me
I will step a little nearer.
. . . Do you see this jeweled headband,
sapphire, emerald, and ruby,
set skillfully in this dull onyx?
Let us in the sapphire's flame
glimpse the Roman Catholic Christian,
in the emerald's glittering prism
every kind of Protestant,
in the ruby's heart the Jew
with his inward-bleeding pain!
But who is there can calculate
the worth of these with certainty?
See! Oh, see! The sun can do it!
Can you see? How clear all shine,
each with the color of their mine
gives the heavenly image back.
Thus the worth of stones is measured

by their power to shine, and not that
of the sun's blaze backward shooting
colored blueish, greenish, red.

And how determine the true worth
among the types of humankind?
Not according to one's faith,
not in language nor in domicile,
these things only are the mine,
only the gem from broken rock
out of which it was rough-hewn,
not its ability to shine.
But the idea of God
and the respect for His commandment
that imbues a soul, just as
when the sun's light fills precious stones
and shines as it journeys on,
truly it permits of nothing
but the true worth of human beings
to be tested and adjudged.

Such souls, wherever they are found,
widespread yet in communion form
the invisible and true
and with heaven's help, unite
in the Lord's own congregation.
And the limbs, when they support
each other, even though disguised
in kaftan or in monk's cowl,
with the passwords "Peace!
Tolerance!"
know at once they have met a member
of the true congregation.

ROSALIE
Away with prejudice! Constance, I think
I shall choose this very spot.

CONSTANCE
From grave to grave the flowers entwine
the garlands of their stems,
as if they seek to prove
that from them we of humankind
should learn such tolerance
and that the churchyard should be the last
of all places upon earth
(for its very name protects it)
to host the conflicts of belief.

JEWESS
True! in these flower-decked graves
that is precisely what we see.
But shall the flames and the sword,
or the keen sharp blade of time,
with the poisoned hate of scorn
keep raging on outside the fence?
Is not the entire globe
no other than a churchyard?
The seeds of tribes dwelt therein
before time ever counted years;
and howe'er widespread they be
in the thousands of the millions,
each life is but a mere leaf,
and at every second rains
a thousand down from its four crowns
over all earth's countless acres.

And for whom—whether Jew
or Christian—is life any more
than uncertain hours of furlough
(in which they can find the Creator
and light the torch of understanding)
from that house which is prepared,
from our hour of birth, *beneath,*
from its inner chamber: the coffin?

Therefore all ought to remember
that where'er they may find themselves
every day their feet will tread
on their own last resting place:
and that on the thin membrane of earth
they steadily consume the seconds
that they live so merrily
until in the midst of pleasure
come what may it breaks apart;
and all of them, although a soul
can with a pool of light illumine
the human being formed of dust,
must obey the sun's timekeeping,
sadly go from morn to evening
circling only, as in chains
round about their own graves.

Then it may be that to their neighbor,
spellbound in the selfsame grip,
they would offer much more love
        on the outside
in that great and widespread churchyard—
        in that garden
where the roads of life are crossing
but which lies in death's dominion.

Translated by Anne Born.

The Thistledown Gatherer
Noli desperare!

Look at the immense and restless red sea of the wide thistle heath!
Like the foam of the stormy ocean spray, the down flies from
countless heads that now, as if in despair over their withering, fade
and fall into the depths. Fresh millions shoot up, tumbling flaming
waves before the wind.

～

Did not a gray-haired farmer sow that field with blessings, and make
the sign of the cross over it? Can curses grow from such seed?

～

But look, out of the sea of thistles a boy's head appears, like someone
drowning! He went out at daybreak to destroy his father's enemies,
the thousands of boastful coppery thistle helmets, and to pick their
down for his grandmother's pillow.

～

The little hero! How he mows and works! He doesn't seem to feel the
rays of the climbing sun. They must be cool in contrast to his love.
His gaze ranges over the heath persistently. He wants to plunder all
the riches of white down before evening comes and the old man seeks
his bed. The thorns are red with his blood. He forges on although at
each step he might set his foot on the swollen coils of a snake beneath
the dense foliage.

～

Already the midday sun has risen high above the woods. The shadow
has grown behind him like the courage of the coward who thinks he

is unnoticed; and still he sees the heath swaying with thistles around the small circle he has cleared.

~

Alas, that too seems to have vanished like a swirl in the ocean. The afternoon breeze lifts fresh thousands into the air, like slaves bold in their numbers. He lets his hands sink down. The wind carries away most of his gains, and blows a new snowdrift into his face.

~

Ah! Equally fruitless are the efforts of charity to combat suffering, which is abundant as the vices whose innumerable thistleheads cause it, so the world of souls is like this heath, filled with millions flowering and fading. Such wild growth in these human souls! Let Death reap this paradise!

~

Strangers' sorrows must be as the flying thistledown, well worth the trouble of turning one's back on! Only one angel has stayed faithful to man: the wingless indifferent ones, with dead eyes, fat cheeks and complacent smile, like all angels except Raphael's, are painted in the churches. He will lead you past suffering with averted eyes, as if past a cursed pillar of salt. All your strength attempting to lighten it would only be like the arms of a child, flung around the pillar in order to move it.

~

Look, the heavens are vaulted high above Earth! Should that bliss be disturbed by the cries of its woe, the rattle of its folly? Rejoice in the beauty of the fields; but forget, that ragged poverty plowed them! Admire the towering strength of castles; but do not feel they are the helmets on the red heads of tyranny!

~

Ah, surely Grandmother's love will fill the rest of the boy's ever hungry bag, in which the down was to be gathered? Its riches have diminished to the size of a snowball; but she will take the weeping boy to her heart and place the down beneath her head and say it has breathed heavenly sleep about her limbs.

◊

So work on with courage, like the boy in the thistle field! His eyes wished to gather in all of it, although his arms only stretched to a circle as wide as their own length after a whole day's work. God does not calculate more than the will. When your cheek glows with righteous anger, other angels than that elusive seed will come, as if at a lighted signal, as if the flaming glance of sympathy was a secret sign between the souls and the heavenly beings. Those same will come who in Gethsemane wiped away the bloody sweat, and kneeling will gather the drops from your brow to become stars in that heaven where your spirit shall dwell and whence the grim burden of your workdays will seem like distant vineyards glittering in the sun.

Originally translated by I. Grøndahl.

Translator's Note

It has been a privilege to work on these translations.

It is never easy to render older writings into modern English, but I have tried to approximate the style and, most importantly, the tone of the original poems from one of Norway's most eminent poets.

I have made use of some earlier translations from the 1920s, by I. Grøndahl and G. M. Gathorne-Hardy, in most cases with considerable alterations, in one or two staying with a good deal of the first translation. If this seems strange, it is a fact that new translations are necessary so that the linguistic changes that develop over time can be drawn on. A tired, out-dated style in the translation can ruin a reader's appreciation of great work.

Professor Frankie Shackelford of Augsburg University very kindly read the translations and made helpful suggestions.

Anne Born

On the importance of this work

"This timeless poetry has relevance and an important message, not least in our own time."
—*Michael Melchior, Deputy Foreign Minister of Israel, 2001–2002; Chief Rabbi of Norway*

"Henrik Wergeland (1808–1845) is one of Norway's greatest poets and was one of the main figures in Scandinavian Romanticism. In two collections of wonderful poetry [translated here], he used his gifts as an artist in the struggle for tolerance and humanitarian values. This English translation of Wergeland's poems on the plight of the Jews will make his struggle known to a broader readership and give the rest of the world access to some of the greatest poems in Norwegian and Scandinavian literature."
—*Vigdis Ystad, Department of Literature, University of Oslo*

"Henrik Wergeland's battle on behalf of the admission of Jews to Norway and for the equality of man clearly had a decisive significance for the Jews who wished to settle in Norway, but it also was of great importance to Norway's reputation as a civilized, cultured state. As a fighter for freedom, Wergeland was a shining example to his contemporaries and a guiding light for the ages."
—*Jo Benkow, president of the Norwegian Parliament, 1985–1989 and 1989–1993*

"One hundred and fifty years ago, on June 13, 1851, the Norwegian Parliament repealed the Constitution's infamous Article 2, known as the 'Jewish Article.' Henrik Wergeland fought tirelessly for its repeal—he regarded it as a stain on Norway—and the fight was won

after his death. The Jews who have lived in Norway since constitute, in a sense, Wergeland's heritage."
—*Mona Levin, journalist*

"Today we face new challenges to how we welcome human beings who are threatened and persecuted. Thus the poetry of Henrik Wergeland is of very great current interest, as a measure of value and a guideline in how we treat our fellow beings. Translating his poems into English will emphasize even more the universality of his message."
—*Rosemarie Köhn, Bishop of Hamar, the Norwegian Church*

"Henrik Wergeland is a national icon. A prolific writer, he fought for tolerance and the rights of the individual."
—*Francis Sejersted, Department of History, University of Oslo; chairman of The Norwegian Nobel Committee, 1991–1999*

"Norway's greatest Romantic poet, Henrik Wergeland, was a leading force behind the nation building in the first half of the 19ᵗʰ century. He held onto an optimistic faith in humanity and its potential for development. His vision for humanity gave rise to the conviction that the provision prohibiting the admission of Jews to the Kingdom was a disgrace to the Constitution, and he fought for change in his writing and public speeches."
—*Barthold Halle, stage director and writer*

"Henrik Wergeland's battle to expunge the Constitution of an injurious article prohibiting Jews admission to the Kingdom employed words as its weapon and has left its mark on our history. When Hitler occupied the country in 1940–1945, Wergeland's view of humanity inspired some of Norway's youth to help save half of Norway's Jewish population from the Holocaust, often putting their own lives at peril. To this day, his humanist credo has acted as a guideline for the best ideas and actions in our nation."
—*Magne Skjæraasen, author and columnist in* Aftenposten *(Norway's leading newspaper)*

"Henrik Wergeland has a place in the heart of every Norwegian thanks to his popular poems and his role in giving this country a day of national celebration in honor of the Constitution, freedom and community. Were racism and xenophobia to sneak their way into this country again, the works of Wergeland would be our first literary weapon against them."
—*Berge R. Furre, Department of Theology, University of Oslo*

"Wergeland contributed significantly to Norway's respect for human rights and the dignity of the individual. Today we are in great need of adequate translations of his works so that his message may reach the world."
—*Egil A. Wyller, Department of Philosophy, University of Oslo*

As an engaged citizen and author in a Christian country, Henrik Wergeland sought to understand and appreciate both his own and other beliefs and traditions. His defense of the rights of Jews was not merely a political stand, but also a theological and religious one— another reason why Henrik Wergeland's legacy continues to have contemporary importance.
—*Henrik Syse, International Peace Research Institute; Department of Political Science, University of Oslo*

Ragnhild Galtung has worked at the American-Scandinavian Foundation in New York and as a director and honorary member of the Norway-America Association in Oslo, Norway. Since 1963 she has been Thanks to Scandinavia's representative in Norway.

Anne Born is an accomplished author and poet and one of the preeminent translators of Scandinavian languages. For this edition, she has reworked several older translations by G. M. Gathorne-Hardy and I. Grøndahl and translated many of Wergeland's poems for the first time.

Dagne Groven Myhren is professor of Norwegian literature at the University of Oslo, Norway. She has done extensive research and published numerous papers on Henrik Wergeland's poetry.